FILE FORMATS 18
MOVIE RECORDING SIZE 19

04 OTHER HELPFUL SETTINGS

DISPLAY SIMULATION 21
PICTURE STYLES 22
CUSTOM WHITE BALANCE 22
COLOR SPACE 23
NOISE REDUCTION 23
AUTO ISO 24
EXPOSURE BRACKETING 24
WIRELESS CONNECTION 25
RESET CAMERA 25

05 STEP-BY-STEP SHOOTING INSTRUCTIONS

HDR 26
TIME-LAPSE MOVIES 27

06 TYPICAL SHOOTING SCENARIOS

PORTRAIT 29
GROUP PORTRAIT 30
LANDSCAPE 32
FREEZE ACTION 33
SHOWING MOTION—PANNING 35
LOW-LIGHT ACTION 36
LONG EXPOSURE 37
MACRO/CLOSE-UP 38
VIDEO RECORDING/VLOGGING 39

01 PRE-SHOOT CHECKLIST

Check these settings before you head out with your camera!

SETTING	MY PREFERRED SETTING
☑ Shooting Mode	....
☑ White Balance Setting	....
☑ ISO Setting	....
☑ Exposure Compensation	....
☑ Focus Mode	....
☑ Focus Method	....
☑ Drive Mode	....
☑ Metering Mode	....
☑ Picture Style	....
☑ Bracketing Setting	....
☑ File Format: JPEG/HEIF, or RAW & JPEG/HEIF	....
☑ Battery Fully Charged and In Camera	....
☑ Memory Card Formatted and In Camera	....

02 BUTTONS, DIALS, AND SCREENS

CAMERA BODY TOP

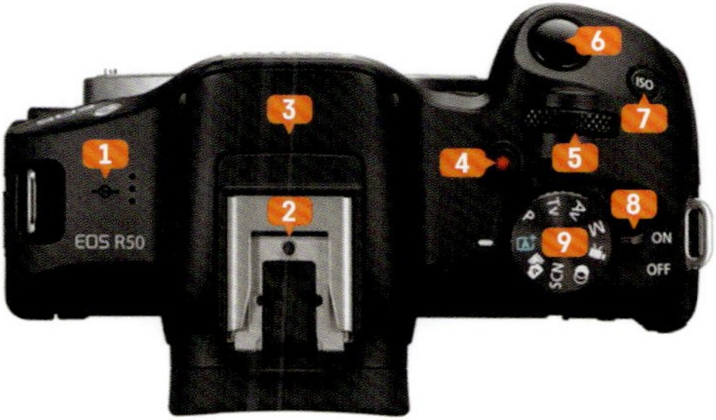

1. **Speaker:** When playing back movies, turn the Main dial to adjust the speaker volume.
2. **Multi-Function Shoe:** External flash units and other accessories can be mounted here.
3. **Built-In Flash:** Open flash manually by pulling up on the front of the flash.
4. **Movie Shooting Button:** Press to start recording a movie.
5. **Main Dial:** Use this dial to set the shutter speed, aperture, and other settings.
6. **Shutter Button:** Press halfway to activate autofocus, press all the way to take the photo.

7. **ISO Button:** Press and rotate main dial to set ISO.
8. **Power Switch:** Turns the camera on and off.
9. **MODE Dial:** Turn the dial to select the Shooting mode.

CAMERA BODY BACK

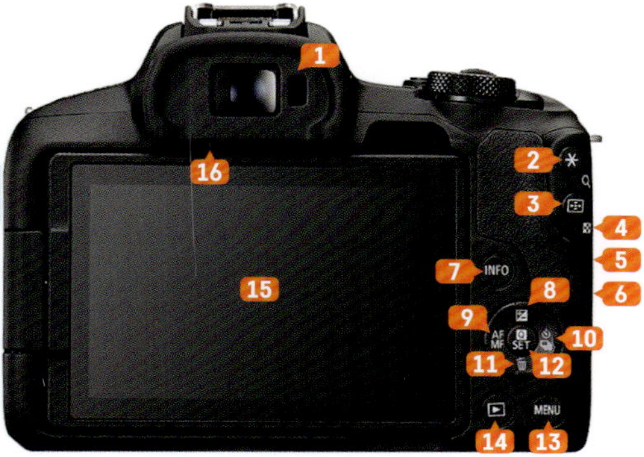

1. **Viewfinder Sensor:** Senses when you're looking through the viewfinder and activates the viewfinder display.
2. **AE Lock / FE Lock / Magnify Button:** When pressed, it locks the exposure / locks the flash exposure when using the flash / zooms into photo during review.
3. **AF Point Selection / Index / Reduce Button:** Press to pick AF point / show the index of images on the memory card / zoom out on a selected image.
4. **HDMI Out (under cover on side):** HDMI micro connection used to output video. The resolution of the HDMI out can be set between Auto and 1080p at Menu > Setup (screen 3) > HDMI Resolution.

5. **Digital Terminal (under cover on side):** USB C terminal used to connect the camera to a computer.
6. **DC Cord Hole (on side):** Plug cord in here to power the camera.
7. **INFO Button:** Press to cycle through views displaying different information.
8. **Up/Exposure Compensation Button:** Used to navigate menus and select or change options / set exposure compensation.
9. **Left/Autofocus/Manual Focus Button:** Used to navigate menus and select or change options / select focusing mode.
10. **Right/Self-Timer/Drive Mode Selection Button:** Used to navigate menus and select or change options / set drive mode.
11. **Down/Erase Button:** Used to navigate menus and select or change options / erases photo or movie on screen during playback.
12. **Quick Control (Q) / Setting (SET) Button:** Use to access the Quick Control screen / finalize a setting and return to a previous screen.
13. **MENU Button:** Press to bring up Menu options.
14. **Playback Button:** Press to view the last image / movie taken.
15. **Screen:** Displays multiple features, options, and settings for shooting and playback.
16. **Diopter Adjustment Slider:** Use to adjust viewfinder focus depending on eyesight.

CAMERA BODY FRONT

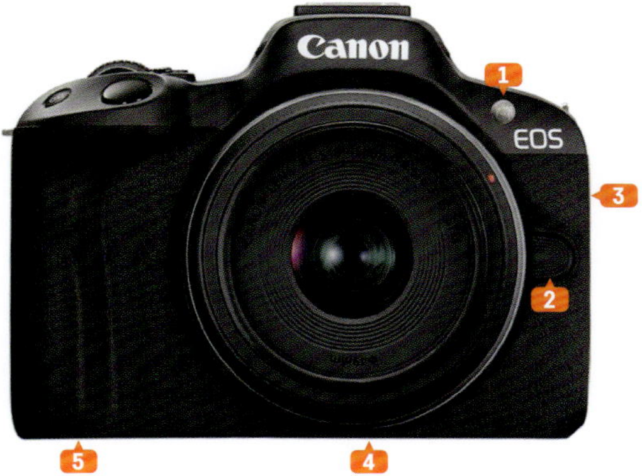

1. AF-Assist Beam/Self-Timer/Remote Control Lamp: Lights up the area in front of the camera in low light/Blinks when Self-Timer is active/Shows when remote is attached.

2. Lens Release Button: Press to remove lens.

3. External Microphone Terminal (under cover on side): Connect external microphone to camera.

4. Tripod Socket: Standard socket for a tripod or monopod.

5. Battery/Memory Card: Open to access the battery and memory card compartment.

SHOOTING SCREEN (STILL PHOTO)

Each time you press the INFO button, the information display will change. The display will show only the settings currently applied.

Note: Viewfinder display positions will vary for some items.

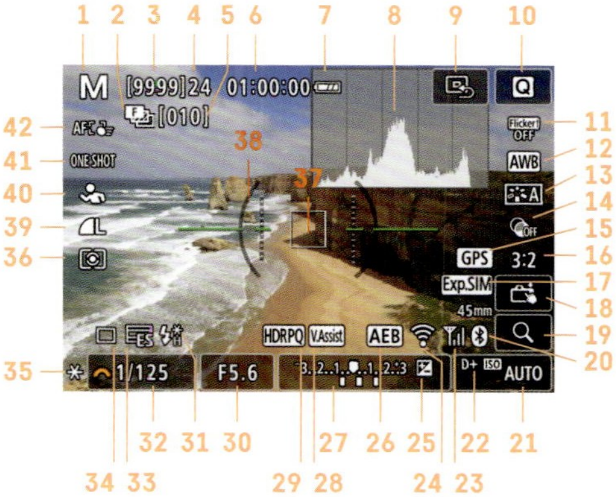

1. **Shooting Mode**
2. **Focus Bracketing / HDR / Multi Shot Noise Reduction**
3. **Number of Available Shots / Self-Timer Countdown**
4. **Maximum Burst**
5. **Remaining Shots for Focus Bracketing**
6. **Movie Recording Time Available**
7. **Battery Level**
8. **Histogram**

9. Reset AF Point to Center Position
10. Quick Control Button
11. Anti-Flicker Shooting
12. White Balance
13. Picture Style
14. Creative Filters
15. GPS
16. Still Image Aspect Ratio
17. Exposure Simulation
18. Touch Shutter
19. Magnify button
20. Bluetooth
21. ISO
22. Highlight Tone Priority
23. Wi-Fi Signal
24. Wi-Fi Function
25. Exposure Compensation
26. AEB/FEB
27. Exposure Level Indicator
28. View Assist
29. HDR PQ
30. Aperture
31. Flash Ready / FE Lock / High-Speed Sync
32. Shutter Speed
33. Electronic Shutter
34. Drive Mode
35. AE Lock
36. Metering Mode
37. AF Point
38. Electronic Level
39. Image Quality
40. Subject to Detect
41. AF Operation
42. AF Area

SHOOTING SCREEN (MOVIE)

Each time you press the INFO button, the information display will change. The display will show only the settings currently applied.

Note: Viewfinder display positions will vary for some items.

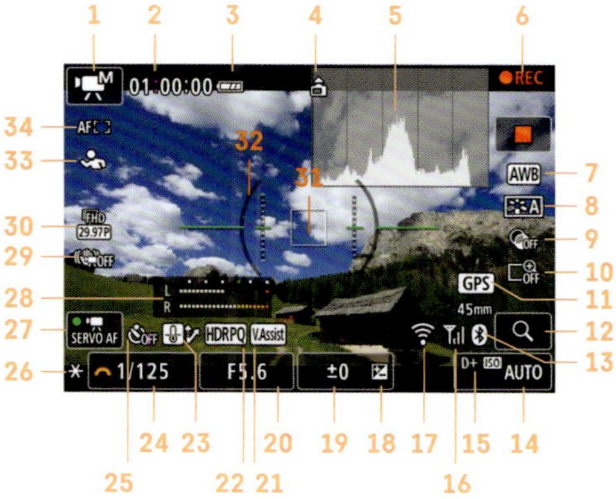

1. **Shooting Mode**
2. **Movie Recording Time / Elapsed Recording Time**
3. **Battery Level**
4. **Shows Current Camera Orientation**

5. **Histogram**
6. **Movie Recording in Progress**
7. **White Balance**
8. **Picture Style**
9. **Creative Filters**
10. **Digital Zoom**
11. **GPS**
12. **Magnify Button**
13. **Bluetooth**
14. **ISO**
15. **Highlight Tone Priority**
16. **Wi-Fi Signal Strength**
17. **Wi-Fi Function**
18. **Exposure Compensation**
19. **Exposure Level Indicator**
20. **Aperture**
21. **View Assist**
22. **HDR PQ**
23. **Overheat Control**
24. **Shutter Speed**
25. **Movie Self-Timer**
26. **AE Lock**
27. **Movie Servo AF**
28. **Audio Level Recording Indicator (manual)**
29. **Movie Digital IS**
30. **Movie Recording Size**
31. **AF Point**
32. **Electronic Level**
33. **Subject to Detect**
34. **AF Area**

03 ESSENTIAL MODES AND SETTINGS

SHOOTING MODES

Rotate the Mode Dial to select a shooting mode.

Creative Zone:

- **P (Program AE):** The camera sets the shutter speed and aperture based on metering info and current ISO.
- **Tv (Time Value, or Shutter Speed Priority):** You set the shutter speed and the camera sets the aperture based on metering info and current ISO.
- **Av (Aperture Value, or Aperture Priority):** You set the aperture and the camera sets the shutter speed based on metering info and current ISO. Range of available apertures depends on the attached lens.
- **M (Manual):** You set ISO, shutter speed, and aperture.

Basic Zone:

- **A+ (Scene Intelligent Auto):** The camera assesses the scene and sets the optimum settings automatically. It will even adjust the focus on both still and moving subjects.
- **A (Hybrid Auto):** You can create a short movie of your photos by shooting just still images. The camera automatically records a 2-4 second clip each time you take a photo. These are later combined into a movie clip.
- **SCN (Special Scene Mode):** You select the proper scene from the list of 14 options and the camera adjusts the settings accordingly.
- **Creative Filters Mode:** This mode allows you to pick one of the creative filters to be applied to your content as its being shot.

Movie Zone:

- **Movie Recording:** Used to take movies. See next section, Movie Shooting Modes.

Note: The Shooting menu options change depending on which shooting zone is selected.

MOVIE SHOOTING MODES

Rotate the Mode dial to Movie Recording, then Menu > Shooting [Screen 1] > Shooting Mode.

Movie Auto Exposure: Camera sets the exposure and ISO.

Movie Manual Exposure: You pick the shutter speed, aperture, and ISO.

Close-Up Demo Movie Recording: Designed for demonstrations, product reviews, and anything happening close the camera. This give priority to things closer to the camera—no AF points are displayed and subjects cannot be manually selected.

Image Stabilization Movie Recording: Select the image stabilization movie mode, then press the AE lock button to select the IS mode. You can select On (applies standard stabilization); Enhanced (applies the most image stabilization); Auto Level (works to keep images horizontal during movie recording); or Off.

HDR Movie Recording: Records movies using a higher dynamic range to keep details in both the shadows and the highlights. Since this mode uses multiple frames merged together, it can produce distorted video, especially when shooting handheld.

Custom Shooting Mode: Uses the settings in the Menu > Set-up (Screen 5) > Custom Shooting Mode (C mode).

METERING MODES

Use shooting menu > Metering mode.

Evaluative: General-purpose mode suited for most situations and subjects (even backlit subjects).

Partial: Uses a medium area at the center of the screen for determining exposure. Good choice when there is very bright light around the subject.

Spot: Uses a small area at the center of the screen. Use when you need to meter on a specific part of the scene.

Center-Weighted Average: The camera analyzes the whole scene to determine exposure, but places more emphasis on info at the center of the screen.

EXPOSURE COMPENSATION

Press the Shutter button halfway down, then press the Up Arrow/Exposure Compensation button and use the main Command Dial to set the compensation, from −3 (darker) to +3 (lighter) stops, in 1/3-stop increments.

Note: The exposure compensation you set will remain in effect until you change it.

FOCUS OPERATION

MENU > AF (Screen 1) > AF Operation > AF

One Shot AF: Focus starts when the Shutter button is pressed halfway, then locks when focus is achieved. Best for stationary subjects.

AI focus: Automatically switches between One Shot and Servo AF depending on the subject.

Servo: Focus starts when Shutter button is pressed halfway and continues to focus until the photo is taken. Best for moving subjects.

Note: For **Manual focus** on lenses with a focus mode switch, set the AF/MF switch on the lens to MF, and rotate the focus ring on the lens barrel to focus. For RF lenses without a focus mode switch, use Menu > AF (Screen 1) > Focus Mode > MF.

AUTOFOCUS AREA

MENU > AF (Screen 1) > AF Area

Spot AF: The smallest possible focusing point, even smaller than 1-Point AF for critical focus.

1-Point AF: The camera focuses using a single point AF.

Expand AF Area: The camera uses one AF point, as well as the points adjacent and nearby to that focus point to help focus. Helpful for moving subjects that are difficult to track with 1-Point AF.

Expand AF Area Around: The camera creates an even larger area around one AF point to find focus.

Flexible Zone AF (1, 2, 3): The camera automatically picks focus using a square set of AF points (1), or a vertical set of AF points (2), or a horizontal set of points (3) using a larger AF area. Generally this will focus on the nearest subject.

Whole Area AF: The camera basically uses the whole focusing area and then decides what to focus on.

Note: Pressing the shutter button halfway down will show which AF points are in focus.

ADDITIONAL AUTOFOCUS OPTIONS

Whole Area Tracking Servo AF: When set to ON, the AF area switches to whole-area AF to track subjects across the whole frame while the shutter button is pressed halfway down. When set to OFF, the subjects are only tracked within the AF points if the shutter button is pressed halfway down (or all the way down).

Subject to Detect: You pick what the camera focuses on. Pick between the following:

- **Auto:** Automatically picks the main subject from any people, animals, or vehicles in the scene.
- **People:** Prioritizes the heads and faces of people. If they can't be tracked, it tracks the torso, and then any other body parts.
- **Animals:** Attempts to track, dogs, cats, and birds (and people) as the main subjects.
- **Vehicles:** The camera attempts to track two- and four-wheeled vehicles (will also track people).
- **None:** The camera does not try to track or determine any subject.

Eye Detection: Works to make sure the eye of any person or animal is in focus. When enabled, the camera will place an AF point directly over the eye.

DRIVE MODES

Press the Drive Mode / Right Arrow key. Select the drive mode using the Main Dial.

Single Shooting: The camera takes a single shot every time Shutter button is pressed.

High-Speed Continuous Shooting +: The camera takes up to 15 shots per second using the electronic shutter or 12 shots per second using the electronic 1st-curtain shutter.

High-Speed Continuous Shooting: The camera takes up to 15 shots per second using the electronic shutter or 7.6 shots per second using the electronic 1st-curtain shutter.

Low-Speed Continuous Shooting: The camera takes up to 5 shots per second using the electronic shutter or 3 shots per second using the electronic 1st-curtain shutter.

Self-Timer 10: Sets the self-timer for 10 seconds.

Self-Timer 2: Sets the self-timer for 2 seconds.

Self-Timer Continuous Shooting: Sets the self-timer to start shooing the set number of photos starting in 10 seconds.

Movie Self-Timer: You can set the camera to delay the start of video recording by either 2 or 10 seconds. Set the mode dial to Movie mode, then MENU > Shooting (Screen 4) > Movie Self-Timer and choose Off, 2 seconds, or 10 seconds. When you are ready to start recording, press the movie shooting button and the recording will start after the set time.

WHITE BALANCE

MENU > Shooting (Screen 4) > White Balance

Auto (AWB) setting is best for most situations, as it uses the ambient light color to adjust the white balance for your images. **AWB-W (Auto-White Priority)** is best when you want to reduce a warm color cast. White balance can be set to shift colors warmer, cooler, or keep them accurate. Other settings are all matched to different lighting types. For truest colors, pick the type of lighting being used to illuminate the scene.

FILE FORMATS

MENU > Shooting (Screen 1) > Image Quality. There are three files types used for image storage: RAW, JPEG, and HEIF file types.

RAW/C-RAW (Compact RAW): The RAW data from the image sensor is recorded each time a photo is taken. The C-RAW version is a compressed RAW file that takes up less space. Set the size using the Main Command Dial.

JPEG/HEIF: Decide the size of the JPEG/HEIF (Large, Medium, Small1, and Small2) using the left and right arrow keys.

RAW/JPEG: If you have selected both a RAW and JPEG/HEIF option, the camera saves two files each time the Shutter button is pressed: a RAW file and a JPEG/HEIF file.

MOVIE RECORDING SIZE

To set size, frame rate, and compression: Rotate the Mode dial to Movie Recording, then Menu > Shooting [Screen 1] > Movie recording Size.

4K Movie Recording: Records at 3840x2160 with an aspect ratio of 16x9. Use a memory card with a fast write speed. If the Overheat control warning appears during recording, stop recording and allow the card to cool before removing it. Any frame from a 4K movie recording can be saved as a JPEG still image.

FHD: Records at 1920x1080 with an aspect ratio of 16x9.

119.9 fps, 59.94 fps, or 29.97 fps: These are used when the output is for NTSC television.

100 fps, 50 fps, 25 fps: These are used for when the output is for PAL television.

Compression Method:

- **IPB (Standard):** Compresses multiple frames at a time. Creates a larger file with less playback compatibility.
- **IPB (Light):** Creates smaller file with higher compatibility and allows longer recording times.

Note: The 119.9 fps / 100 fps setting is meant for slow-motion playback and the recording time is limited to

15 minutes. It does not record sound. The movies are actually recorded at 29.9 (25) fps and will playback at 1/4 speed.

Note: All movies are recorded using the MP4 recording format.

Note: When using an SDHC card formatted in the camera, if the movie file exceeds 4GB, a new movie file will be created and start recording automatically. You will have to use software on a computer to edit the movies together. If you use a SDXC card formatted in the camera, you can record more than 4GB per movie.

04 OTHER HELPFUL SETTINGS

DISPLAY SIMULATION

MENU > Shooting (Screen 8) > Display Simulation. This feature displays a simulation of the current exposure settings as they are applied to the scene.

Exposure + DOF: Image brightness and depth of field as displayed tries to closely match the exposure.

Exposure: Image brightness is displayed to match the settings used to take the photo.

Exposure Only During DOF Preview: The image is displayed at normal brightness unless the DOF preview button is pressed; then the display will try to match the settings used.

Disable: The image is displayed at the standard brightness all the time, regardless of exposure settings or exposure compensation.

PICTURE STYLES

MENU > Shooting (Screen 4) > Picture Style

Allows you to adjust settings for JPEG images. Adjustable settings are Sharpness (Strength, Fineness, Threshold), Contrast, Saturation, Color Tone, Filter Effect (Monochrome), and Toning Effect (Monochrome). Seven preset picture controls can all be adjusted: **A (Auto), S (Standard), P (Portrait), L (Landscape), FD (Fine Detail), N (Neutral), F (Faithful), M (Monochrome)**. The Monochrome also has four color filters: Yellow, Orange, Red, Green. Finally, there are also three User-Defined Picture Styles, which allow you to customize any of the styles for easy access.

CUSTOM WHITE BALANCE

Setting a custom White Balance can help you get the best color when you're shooting under mixed lighting:

1. Take a photo of a white card (or white wall) under the mixed lighting at the scene.
2. Select MENU > Shooting (Screen 4) > Custom White Balance.
3. Select the white image taken in step 1 and press the OK button.
4. Select MENU > Shooting (Screen 4) > White Balance, and select the Custom White Balance icon.

COLOR SPACE

MENU > Shooting (Screen 4) > Color Space

sRGB: Smaller color space. Best when images are used directly from camera.

Adobe RGB: Larger color space. Best used when images will be edited with post-processing software.

NOISE REDUCTION

MENU > Shooting (Screen 5) > Long Exposure Noise Reduction

Reduces noise in images with shutter speeds of 1 second or longer. Doubles time needed to save image to memory card. Choices are Auto, Enable, and Disable. Auto is usually the best choice.

MENU > Shooting (Screen 5) > High ISO Speed NR

Reduces noise in images taken at high ISO settings. Use Standard for default, Low for less noise reduction, and High for more noise reduction. There is also the option to use Multi-Shot Noise Reduction—this mode uses four consecutive images combined into a single JPEG with the highest level of noise reduction applied. Cannot be used when the image quality is set to RAW or RAW+JPEG.

AUTO ISO

Press the ISO button and rotate the Main Dial to select an ISO between 100 – 32000 in 1/3 step increments; or set to AUTO.

You can use MENU > Shooting (Screen 2) > ISO Speed Settings to set the maximum ISO the camera will use when set to AUTO ISO.

EXPOSURE BRACKETING

You can bracket a set of three exposures up to +/-3 stops in 1/3-stop increments:

1. Select MENU > Shooting (Screen 2) > Exposure Compensation/AEB.

2. Set the Bracketing range by turning the Main dial.

3. If desired, set the exposure compensation amount by pressing the Cross Keys.

4. Take the pictures, and three bracketed shots will be created. (If you're in Single shooting drive mode, take three pictures to create the bracketed sequence. If you're in a Continuous shooting drive mode, the three shots will be taken together when you press and hold the Shutter button.)

Note: Bracketing will remain on until you set the Bracketing range back to 0.

Note: The three photos will be in the following order: Properly exposed, underexposed, and overexposed.

WIRELESS CONNECTION

Install the Camera Connect app on your smartphone and pair it with the EOS R50.

This will allow you to view and transfer images to your smartphone, see the Live View image on your smartphone, and even shoot remotely from your smartphone.

RESET CAMERA

MENU > Set-Up (Screen 5) > Reset Camera

Pick between Basic Settings, which restores the default settings for camera shooting functions and menu settings; or Other Settings, which allows for individual selected options to be reset.

05 STEP-BY-STEP SHOOTING INSTRUCTIONS

HDR HDR

Combine three images to reduce the contrast and improve tonal range. The Canon R50 generates one JPEG or HEIF image as the resulting HDR image:

1. Select MENU > Shooting (Screen 2) > HDR mode.
2. Choose the range you want:

   Auto: Sets the dynamic range automatically depending on the scene's tonal range.

   +/–1, +/–2, or +/–3: The higher the number, the wider the dynamic range of the image will be.
3. If using the HDR PQ, you can limit the max brightness to 1000 units or keep it set to Disable, which does not limit the brightness.
4. Select an option for Continuous HDR:

   1 Shot Only: You'll only shoot one HDR image.

   Every Shot: You'll keep shooting HDR images until you disable HDR shooting.

5. Select the Auto Image Align setting:

   Enable: Choose this if you're shooting handheld.

   Disable: Choose this if you're shooting on a tripod.

6. Take the picture.

TIME-LAPSE MOVIES

Create a time-lapse movie in-camera:

1. Set the Mode Dial to Movie Mode.
2. MENU > Shooting (Screen 4) > Time-Lapse Movie.
3. Select Scene:

   Scene 1 is for moving subjects like walking people.

   Scene 2 is for slowly moving subjects like clouds.

   Scene 3 is for slowly changing subjects like sunrises or sunsets.

4. Select the Interval using the left and right arrow keys.
5. Set the Number of Shots you'd like to take for the time-lapse movie.
6. Select Auto Exposure to choose the shooting method:

   Fixed 1st Frame: The first shot is metered, then all subsequent shots match that first shot's exposure.

   Each Frame: Each frame is metered and shot separately.

7. In the Screen Auto Off option, choose Disable to have the image displayed (though the screen will automatically turn off 30 minutes after the time-lapse shooting begins); choose Enable to have the screen turn off 10 seconds after the time-lapse shooting begins.

Note: You can press the INFO button at any time during time-lapse shooting to turn the screen on and off.

8. Choose whether you'd like to hear a beep after every image is captured (Beep per Image Taken).

9. Once all these settings are selected, press MENU to turn off the menu screen.

10. A message on screen will prompt you to take a few test shots.

11. Press the Movie Shooting button, then press the Shutter button to start shooting the time-lapse movie.

06 TYPICAL SHOOTING SCENARIOS

SHOOTING SCENARIO
PORTRAIT

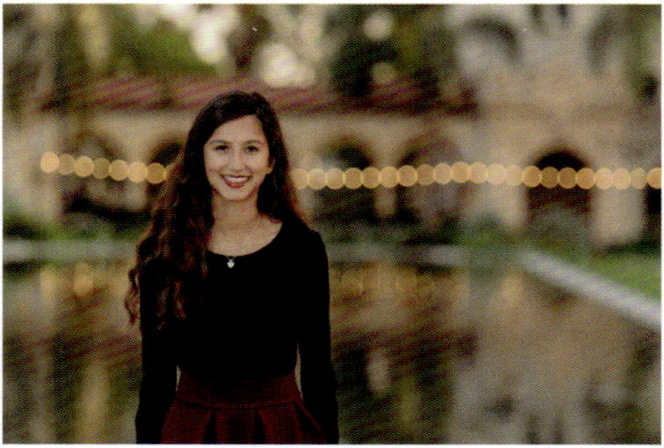

KEY PRINCIPLES

- The key to a portrait like this is shallow depth of field. So shoot in **APERTURE PRIORITY (Av)** mode and start with the lowest aperture your lens offers (such as **f/2.8 or f/4**).
- Remember to **focus on the eyes**.
- If the image is too dark or too light, use **EXPOSURE COMPENSATION** to adjust the brightness level.

- If the image is blurry from a slow shutter speed, **raise the ISO** to increase your sensor's sensitivity to light, thus allowing for a faster shutter speed.
- Remember to use a **focal length of 50mm or greater** so that you don't distort your subject's face.

SHOOTING SCENARIO
GROUP PORTRAIT

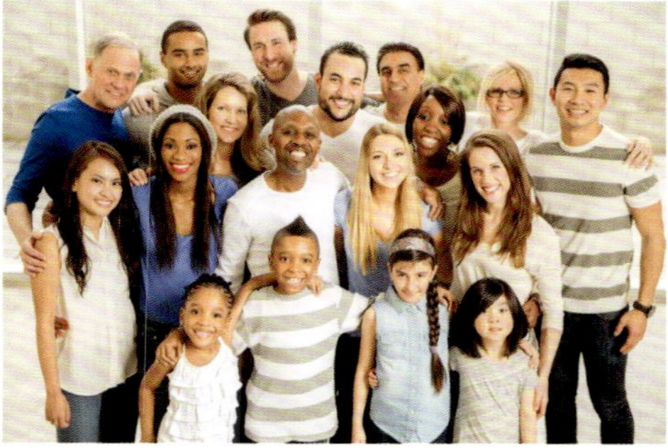

KEY PRINCIPLES

- In order to get everyone in focus, you need a deep depth of field. So shoot in **APERTURE PRIORITY (Av)** mode and set the aperture between **f/8–f/16**.
- **Focus on the person in the middle of the group.** Check the focus by using the LCD screen. View it at 100% and check faces in the front and back rows. If anyone is out of focus, use a smaller aperture for deeper depth of field.
- Use **EVALUATIVE METERING** to account for the light in the entire scene.
- **Arrange the group so they can all see you** (and you can see them).
- Use **EXPOSURE COMPENSATION** if the image is too bright or too dark.
- If image is blurry, **raise the ISO** to allow the camera to use a faster shutter speed.

SHOOTING SCENARIO
LANDSCAPE

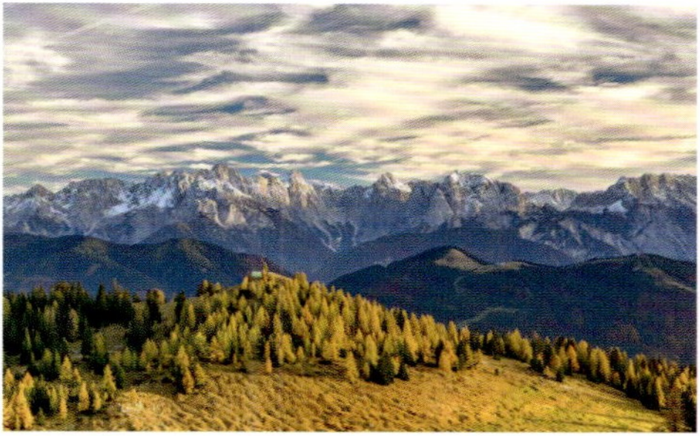

KEY PRINCIPLES

- Shoot in **APERTURE PRIORITY (Av) mode** to control depth of field, and start with **f/16** to ensure deep depth of field.
- **Use a tripod** to eliminate camera movement. Whenever your camera is on a tripod, also make sure that any **IMAGE STABILIZATION** is turned off.
- Use **EVALUATIVE METERING** and **ONE SHOT AF** focus mode.

- **Set the ISO to a low setting (100–200)** to avoid any digital noise.
- Shoot in **RAW** so that you have the most available information when editing later.
- Consider **BRACKETING** your exposures.

SHOOTING SCENARIO
FREEZE ACTION

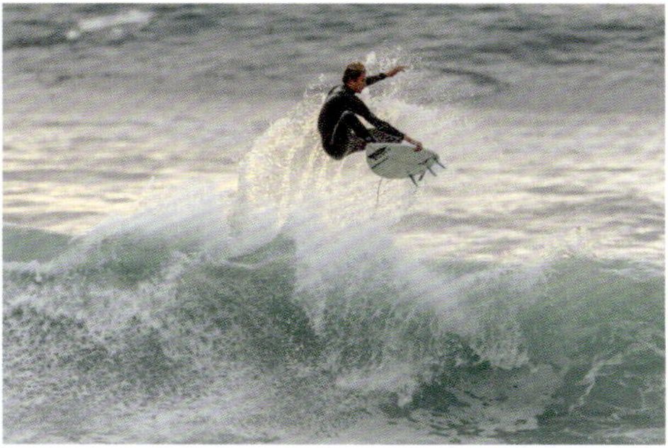

KEY PRINCIPLES

- Use **SHUTTER PRIORITY (Tv)** mode and set the shutter speed to a value that will freeze the action. The appropriate shutter speed depends on your subject and its movement, but could be anywhere between **1/500–1/4000 sec** (1/8000 if you are using the electronic shutter).
- Use High-Speed Continuous Shooting +: This shoots in the highest frame rate and will help capture the fast action.
- Use **SERVO** autofocus so that the camera keeps focusing as the subject moves.
- If the image is dark or blurry, **raise the ISO** or try AUTO ISO to automatically have the camera adjust the ISO as needed.

SHOOTING SCENARIO

SHOWING MOTION—PANNING

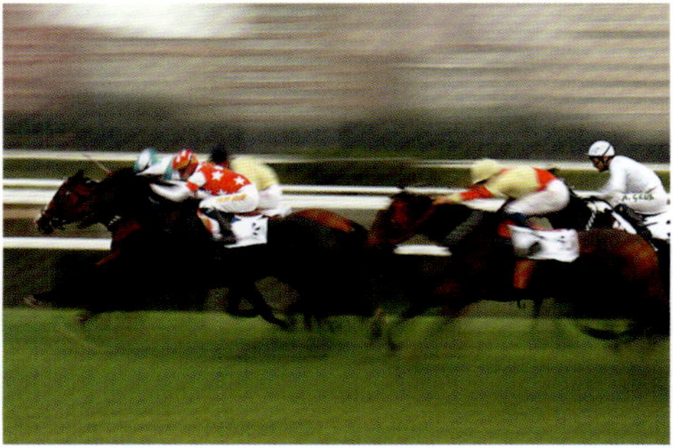

KEY PRINCIPLES

- Shoot in **SHUTTER PRIORITY (Tv)** mode and use a slow-enough shutter speed to allow for the subject to move during the exposure.
- **Follow the subject** across the frame as you shoot.
- Use **SERVO** autofocus, as well as the **EXPAND AF AREA** focus mode to ensure the camera focuses on the subject.

SHOOTING SCENARIO

LOW-LIGHT ACTION

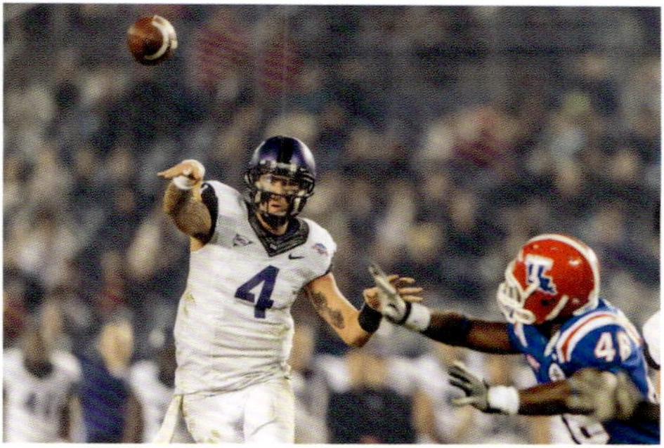

KEY PRINCIPLES

- Shoot in **APERTURE PRIORITY (Av)** mode and use a wide aperture such as **f/2.8 or f/4**.
- Use **PARTIAL METERING** and meter on the subject's face.
- Use **SERVO** autofocus and **1-POINT AF** (a single focus point).
- **Set the ISO to 1600 or higher**, depending on the amount of available light.
- If the image is blurry, **increase the ISO** to allow for a faster shutter speed.

SHOOTING SCENARIO

LONG EXPOSURE

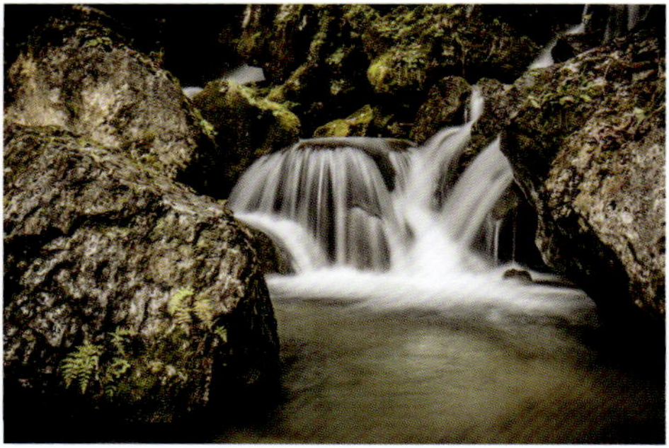

KEY PRINCIPLES

- Use **MANUAL** shooting mode, which allows you to use the **BULB** shutter speed for long exposures.
- **Use a tripod** to keep the camera stable.
- Use the **ONE SHOT AF** focus mode, or try manual focus if the camera is having a hard time locking on focus.
- **Use a low ISO** (100–400) and **shoot RAW** to ensure a high-quality file.
- Use a **remote release** with a lock to avoid touching (shaking) the camera.

SHOOTING SCENARIO

MACRO/CLOSE-UP

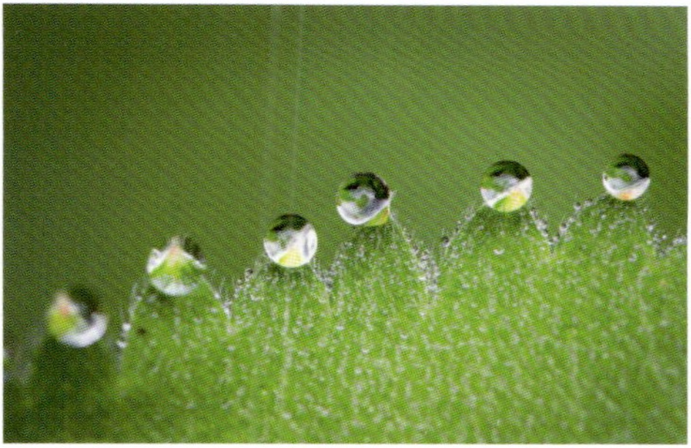

KEY PRINCIPLES

- Shoot in **APERTURE PRIORITY (Av)** mode and **use a small aperture** to ensure you achieve enough depth of field (this image was shot at f/13).
- Use **EVALUATIVE METERING** to analyze the light in the entire frame.
- A **tripod** is very useful for keeping the camera steady.

- Use **MANUAL FOCUS** and **zoom in** to confirm your focus is tack-sharp.
- Try using a dedicated **macro lens** or **close-up filters** to make sure you can achieve sharp focus when you're so close to the subject.

SHOOTING SCENARIO

VIDEO RECORDING/VLOGGING

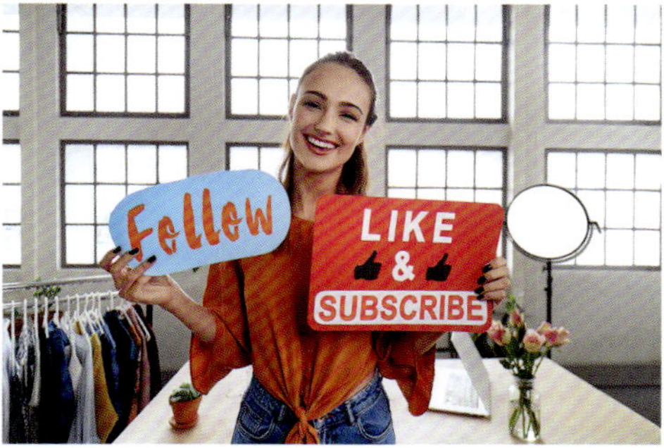

KEY PRINCIPLES

- Use a **shallow depth of field** to keep the viewers' attention on the subject. A **wide aperture** will keep the subject in focus while having the area in front of and behind the subject fall out of focus.
- Use **24 fps** for a more cinematic look.
- Set the **shutter speed** to **twice the frame rate**, or as close as you can get. If using 24 fps, the shutter speed should be 1/50 (or 1/60) second.
- Use an **external microphone** for better sound. The Rode VideoMic GO II is a great starter microphone.
- Keep the camera stable with a **tripod or gimble**. Smooth footage looks more professional.
- Use the **swing-out monitor** to watch the video being recorded. Remember to leave a second of two of nothing at the beginning and end of your video clips—this will make them much easier to edit later.

OM SYSTEM "OLYMPUS" OM-3

POCKE

TABLE OF CONTENTS

01 PRE-SHOOT CHECKLIST

02 BUTTONS, DIALS, AND SCREENS

CAMERA BODY TOP ....

CAMERA BODY FRONT ....

CAMERA BODY BACK ....

VIEWFINDER/LIVE VIEW SCREEN ....

SUPER CONTROL PANEL/LIVE VIEW SUPER CONTROL PANEL ....

03 ESSENTIAL MODES AND SETTINGS

SHOOTING MODES 10

METERING MODES 11

EXPOSURE COMPENSATION 12

FOCUS MODES 12

AUTOFOCUS TARGET MODES 13

DRIVE MODES 14

WHITE BALANCE 16

IMAGE SIZE/QUALITY 17

04 OTHER HELPFUL SETTINGS **18**

CREATIVE DIAL 18

PICTURE MODES 19